# JUST
# START
# IT !

**Louise Nunga**

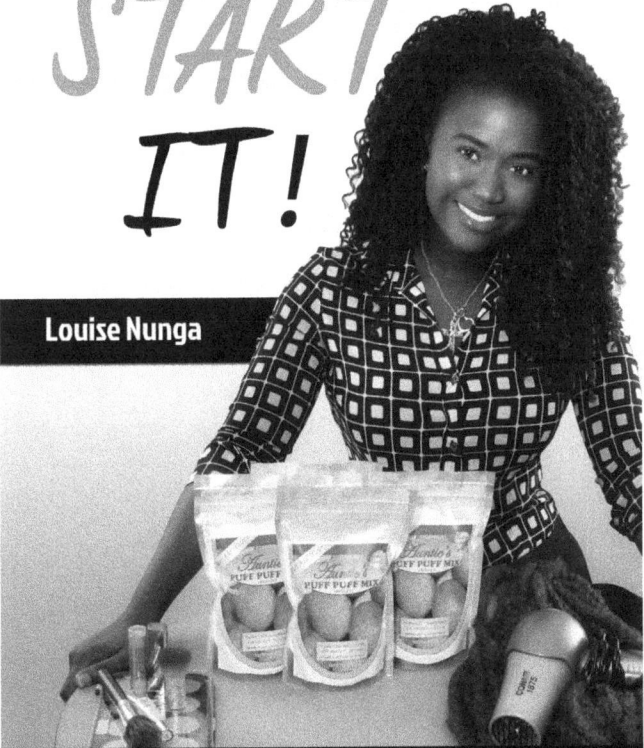

## Activating Your God-Gifted Business

# Just Start It!

## Activating Your God-Gifted Business

**Louise Nunga**

Anointed Fire House
www.anointedfirehouse.com

# Dedication

This book is dedicated to the Holy Spirit for inspiration and instructions, to Jesus Christ for giving me life through Him, and God, the Father, for strategizing all things to work out for my good.

# Acknowledgment

I want to thank Tiffany Buckner for planting the seed of me writing a book in my spirit, the father of my children for consistently supporting me in all my business adventures, and to Pastor and Lady Cullen for holding my hand, teaching me how to obey God and yield to hear the Holy Spirit audibly. Thank you Grandma Mbamba, Mom, and Dad for sowing good morals and strength into me. Thank you for teaching me to believe in myself. My sister, Carene, Uncle Tata and Uncle Daniel for being my biggest fans, giving me honest criticism designed to help me become a better person. Lastly, thank you to every family member, friend, and client who've asked and listened to my business advice and acted on it. It gave me the confidence I needed to believe that I can add the title " author" to my resume.

# Table of Contents

# Introduction

Most people want to be their own boss, but they don't know where to start. God placed the spirit of creativity in all of us, but of the more than three hundred million people in the United States, only 27 million are entrepreneurs. That's less than ten percent of all Americans! Sadly enough, these numbers seem to decline in other countries, given the fact that the United States, according to the GEI ranking, holds the number one spot for the country with the most entrepreneurs. What's happening in this world? After all, technology continues to get smarter, which means that people are getting smarter. The answer is simple: there are many creative people in this world, but the majority of them are afraid to be more than they're expected to be. What does this mean? It means that the problem isn't a lack of ideas; it's a lack of courage and a lack of encouragement.

In this powerful book, you will come to better understand the heart of entrepreneurship. It's time to stop making excuses and procrastinating with your business, and just start it!

Follow new author, Louise Nunga, as she describes how she turned her ideas into successful businesses. Find out how, through the blood of Jesus, she overcame her fears and contended with doubt, sabotage, self-destruction and everything that dared to stand in her way!

# Chapter 1

# Marriage, Relationships, and Business

## Who you marry, can make or break your business

I meet a lot of younger women and men aspiring to get married. My first advice to them is to make sure you choose a mate who will support and add to your gifted business. All too often, we pick mates based solely on our perception of love, but later on, when we want to operate in our gifts, our mates oppose and shut them down. After you have prayed for a mate, you have to also be watchful. Matthew 26:41 says, "Watch and pray so that you will not fall into temptation. The spirit is willing, but the flesh is weak." When the potential mate shows up, you are responsible for asking yourself if he/she is in alignment with your gifted purpose. The signs are always there. All too often, we choose what we want to see and how we choose to interpret it. For example, if you're an aspiring entertainer and you come across a potential mate who, because of his or her own insecurities, believes that all entertainers are liars, you need to run. That person will kill your gifted purpose. Now, it's different when he or she enjoys quality entertainment and can differentiate which kind of entertainment is productive versus disruptive. There's a difference. Make sure to investigate and dig to find your partner's true intentions.

When I was in college, I dated a guy who was book smart. He was in the medical field, studying to be a Surgeon and wanted a future mate of his caliber. Hence, every time I shared my dreams of starting my own business, he heard nothing but excuses. He believed that I didn't want to work harder in school to be a Pharmacist (which was the field I majored in college). I always joked to my friends about the fact that we couldn't even watch television together. He wanted to watch CNN, while I wanted to watch BET. Of course, some may say that CNN is more educational than BET, and they would be right. However, at that time, I was fascinated with entertainment; it got my creative energy flowing. I wasn't watching it for the dancing; I was looking at how a series or movie was put together. I looked at the behind-the-scenes clips of music videos, amongst other things. The point was, I saw creative business opportunities and he saw people dancing seductively. Needless to say, that relationship ended painfully. It wasn't that I was right or he was wrong. It just wasn't a match for our gifts. Either I would distract him from becoming a gifted Surgeon or he would distract me from going into business.

When I met my ex-husband, I was intrigued by the fact that he fully accepted my creative spirit and dreams. He truly let me be me — **with** integrity. I had to make a few changes to a few of my businesses to ensure that they were in order with our Christian walk, but I wasn't shutdown. For example, I use to be a nightclub promoter. With this business, I had to be in the nightclub scene to oversee things. That had to be adjusted. Instead, I had to learn to do event planning, such as concerts and weddings, amongst other things, to express my talent. One day, while we were dating, I was struggling to find an easy way to fry "puff puff" (an African doughnut snack). I complained, telling him that there wasn't an easy way to make this snack. It required a lot of measurements and timing. My ex responded, "Why don't you create an instant mix and sell it?" That was the birth of "Aunties Puff-Puff Mix". He could have misinterpreted what I said as, "I can't cook," but his creative discernment saw a business opportunity. I gave you insight into my story, so you can have tangible examples and are not confused.

I know a beautiful aspiring actress who had been growing her fan base for years. She wrote scripts and acted in dramatic scenes; she is talented and gorgeous. Her Instagram page grew to over ten thousand followers. One day, she fell in love with a man who did not see business opportunities, he saw her getting a lot of attention and decided that he didn't want to marry her. So, in the name of compromise, she deleted that account and started a new one. Just so we are clear, she didn't have nude or inappropriate pictures on her profile. However, even if she did, a creative mind would have advised her to delete the pictures or videos and rebrand herself. Sometimes, you do have to start totally afresh and tear down all ungodly foundations, but this wasn't the case. He was insecure and threatened by the attention she was getting. Needless to say, that relationship ended.

Your spouse should be a help meet, serving and living in purpose. Most of the time, when we meet our future spouses, we haven't figured out our true purposes in life. That's when fervent prayers come in handy. We are not all-knowing, but He (Jesus Christ) is. Psalms 139:1 says, "O lord you have searched me and have known me…" Men lie and women lie, but Jesus is the  Way, the Truth, and the Life. Choose your mate with guidance from the truth. Think about it — if you don't know your true purpose or gift, how do you make the RIGHT choice? "It's like throwing a dice and hoping for life" (Pastor Raymond Cullens). We will get signs and intuitions on what God is showing us, not just telling us. The only true way of choosing a spouse is through obeying God's will, and to know God's will, we must know His word. If you are a babe in Christ, seek guidance from Christ-like spiritual authorities. This was one of the biggest mistakes I made. Every future couple should have trusted, Godly spiritual parents to counsel them and test both parties to see if God truly put them together. Even with prophecies, you have to test the spirit to see if it is truly from God. How do you test the spirit? 1 Corinthians

14:29 tells us to let two or three people prophesy, and let the others evaluate what is said. You need to have God's authority in your life to evaluate if the prophecy aligns with God's word. And even after you get a yes, there are processes to take before walking down the aisle. It sounds long and complicated, right? It should because this has to do with your life, destiny, and life of your future children. So, no shortcuts!

## Your marriage is your first business; be accountable

Your business is not your first priority on this Earth. Marriage or family should be first. When business is new and growing at a slow pace, we put our family first. Then success and all its demands arrive, and our priorities suddenly shift. We turn our businesses into idols and start worshipping them. True accountability to a spouse helps in keeping us on the right paths. Notice I said "true accountability" — not just accountability, because we sometimes do selective accountability. When we are selective in accountability with our spouses, our ways become crooked and we become liars. We have all heard the adage that says "when you tell a lie, you have to tell more lies to hide the first one." This sounds like a lot of work in its own, right? True accountability means you share all information with your spouse — the person you are sure God sent as your help meet. This means you share all information about money, business partners, employees, and everything regarding your business. You share what business you want to do, who you want to do this with, how you intend to do the business and much more. You share all to ensure your partner gets involved and can guide you every step of the way. However, sharing alone is not true accountability if your intent is not to receive their input. If you do this, you are just giving a report of what you have already decided to do. My ex-husband and I had to learn this lesson the hard way because we didn't know any better. We were doing selective accountability and the devil crept in slowly but surely and created chaos. Thankfully, God decided to turn a mess into a message.

Some people say that they can't tell their spouses how much they really make. This is because they believe their spouses will take advantage of it. I've heard people say that they can't tell their spouses that they are doing business with the opposite sex because they know how their spouses are. If all this is true, there's an underlying issue that needs to be addressed and dealt with. True accountability doesn't work when there are foundational issues in a marriage that haven't been resolved. And adding lies on top of these unresolved issues only creates more issues. I know people who feel that it's okay for them to have secret accounts that their spouses are unaware of. Nothing hides under the sun forever, so imagine how they'll feel and react when they do find out the truth. Honestly, it's just a matter of time before they find out. It will be an unnecessary battle just because they were selective about their accountability. Quite a few marriages have suffered infidelity — a spouse had an affair with a business associate who wasn't accounted for. Your spouse can help you avoid certain temptations when you are truly accountable. True accountability can eliminate a lot of the drama we find our marriages in. This doesn't mean that we won't face storms because all marriages do, but I do believe it would reduce the number of storms.

True accountability aids in eliminating both the inferiority and superiority complex between couples. Inferiority complex is defined as "an unrealistic feeling of general inadequacy caused by actual or supposed inferiority in one sphere, sometimes marked by aggressive behavior in compensation" (Reference: Dictionary.com). Superiority complex is defined as "an attitude of feeling better than others that conceals actual feelings of inferiority and failure" (Reference: Google). These definitions sound stressful and chaotic. With these types of feelings, competition becomes the norm, hence, creating marriages where individuals seek to prove that they can do better than their spouses. Does anyone really want this in marriage? I don't believe so. However, this insidious mindset creeps in slowly but surely over the lifespan of inaccountability. So always choose accountability, even when it's uncomfortable. The gains in the long-run outweigh, by far, the discomfort.

# Chapter 2

# Business Unveils Who You Truly Are

In dealing with the daily activities in your business, you learn a lot about yourself. You learn about your strengths, weaknesses, moralities, integrity, faith and much more. If you want to learn more about yourself, start a business. Owning a business forces you to exercise the muscles of your character. Customers will test the strength of your patience and principles. Over the course of operating as a business owner of multiple businesses, I've learned a lot about myself. I have learned my weaknesses, such as laziness and a tendency to be shallow. I didn't want to wake up early in the mornings (I still don't), so I created hours that served me, not my clients. I had a very low level of patience and understanding. I lacked leadership because my thought process with my team was that we are all grown, so everyone should lead himself or herself. As time went on, I also uncovered my strengths. I am great at activating an idea and bringing it to life with no hesitation or strategic plan. Talking to people about business is an exciting hobby of mine. Learning and education became fun for the first time in all my school years. People are inspired by my ability to be courageous in starting multiple businesses. All this and more was mind-blowing to me. We don't really know our strengths or weaknesses without testing our different personalities.

One day, my company, Mobile Braiders, had a team meeting. This was a culture we had just started and there was a need for my leadership guidance. My plan was to just drop off my cousin who needed a ride to a job interview, and then head to the meeting with my then four-month-old baby in the car. On our way to her interview, my new car broke down. I managed to drive it carefully to the nearest dealership and called an Uber cab to pick her up. While at the dealership, I called my company's manager and asked her to pick me up. She arrived with another team member who was also headed to the meeting. I got in her car calmly and we started heading to the meeting. I was talking about the topics for the meeting and business. She said to me "Louise, I don't know how you deal with all this stress and stay calm; you are strong and patient." I was caught off guard by that statement and flabbergasted by it. The reason being is that I've always seen myself as sensitive, soft and emotional, which are traits that some people consider to be signs of weakness. And patience was not my strength, or so I thought. I gradually realized that my so-called weaknesses had become my strengths over time.

If you are a greedy, money-chasing person deep down inside, this flaw will unveil itself in your entrepreneurial dealings.

Sometimes, because we were never tested with certain elements, we misrepresent who we really are underneath it all. People can be humble when they are broke, but if they receive a million dollars, their true character will reveal itself. Money is not evil; our selfish intentions with money are the real evils. It's easy for some of us to be polite and humble at our jobs because of the fear of termination, but if someone gives us the power to be our own bosses, humility will suddenly become the thing that we have to struggle with. This is to say that business will unveil who we truly are. Needless to say, this can be a great advantage because transformation can only occur after you unveil or meet your true self. Changing for the better won't occur until we've been introduced the worst parts of ourselves.

### Who are you really?

Operating as a business owner will fuel your bad habits and great habits. It's up to you to use the realization of your weaknesses as an advantage. Nothing is new underneath the sun. Whatever weaknesses you have, please know that someone else has overcome and written a book about them. Educate yourself on how to reduce your weaknesses, but don't focus on them. Focusing solely on perfecting your weaknesses will make you less productive. Most of your energy should be on perfecting your strengths. After getting insight on the strengths you lack, you have two paths you can take. Educate yourself to reduce your weaknesses so it's not detrimental to your business. Then, if you can, hire or partner with someone whose strength is your weakness. This process doesn't happen instantaneously; it takes time. Finding the right partner or team takes time to grow and deal with the trials with errors. Reducing your bad habits take time. As long as you are a work in progress, you will be great.

Your personal principles shouldn't be left at home. Bring them with you to your business environment. Honesty and integrity can be principles you value at home with your friends and family. Include these values in your business dealings so you are not living a double life. You can't detest dishonesty at home, yet you're not honest with your customers or business associates. It eventually takes a toll on your being and spirit. Sooner or later, you will get overwhelmed trying to live a double life, and eventually, you'll have to choose one personality. Some have chosen the love of money, and this transformed them into people who their friends can no longer recognize. On the other hand, some have chosen to become better people because they wanted to prevent falling into the snares that have destroyed so many businesses to date.

# Chapter 3

# Just Start it Already!

## Starting is how you start your business

Many people want to start a business, but are unsure of how to start, where to start, what to start and when to start. Every time I'm talking with someone who has this state of mind, my recommendation to them is to "just start" the business and the rest will follow. I know this seems to go against what a lot of us were taught. We were taught that you have to have a business plan, find capital, get a team together and so on. Then and only then, should you start a business. Most people with this mindset NEVER start their businesses. They get stuck in this state of mind, believing that when or if they get everything they need together, they'll then be ready to launch their visions. I have met countless people who are still stuck in this phase, and before you know it, life has passed them by. I have come to realize a very interesting concept in all my research; that is, there is a difference between a successful CEO versus a wanna-be CEO. Ponder on it. A lot of us think about great ideas and solutions to a problem. Sooner or later, we see the very ideas we had being advertised by someone else. We then think to ourselves that we were the originators of that idea or solution, even though we never took the time to give birth to it. The difference is someone took the idea and activated it, and now, that person is making money from it. So, why couldn't that be you? You were smart enough to think about that brilliant idea, which means you do have what it takes.

One of the main reasons I believe so strongly in not waiting is because we will not have our full business plans or visions until we're actively engaged in our new businesses. Facebook started as a platform for college students to socialize. I don't believe Mark

Zuckerberg had the full picture of what it would become today. Facebook makes over 70 percent of its revenue today from advertisements. Most people use it freely, while business owners like myself pay to use Facebook. Can you imagine if Mark Zuckerberg waited until he figured out his purpose? So, in the midst of all the question marks, just start. The rest will be revealed to you and you will grow and mature into it.

## Start with excellence

Please do not misinterpret my passion for encouraging you to just start. Start with excellence. I am equally passionate about excellence as I am with business start-up. Every time I see a business being presented in an unprofessional manner, I flinch. With all the resources available to us now, there's no reason to present your baby in rags. No one respects a well-dressed mother carrying a baby wrapped in rags. Presentation is key in the age we live in. If you present carefully prepared food on the lid a trash can, no one would taste it. I say all this to leave a lasting impression on your mind. In every business move or strategy, think excellence. Excellence doesn't equate to expensive; there's a huge difference. Excellence can be finding cheaper ways or creative do-it-yourself means to present your business. For example, the pictures you use to advertise your product or business should be clear and attractive. You don't have to hire a professional with high-end equipment to shoot your photos. You can use your phone's camera to start. However, have excellence on your mind. If your  phone camera takes very low quality photos, upgrade to a better phone. Most of us can do this these days because of all the options available. If you absolutely can't afford to upgrade your phone, and you must use what you have, be creative. The camera might not take clear pictures in dark areas, and if this is the case, take the shots outside in daylight. This is just an example. I could go on, but I hope you get the point. Always have excellence in mind. Take excellence with you in your business meetings, reflect it in your attire, speech, customer service, social media pages and so on. Always take excellence with you; let her be your best friend, never leave her at home. There's always a creative way to be excellent. I have listed a directory of excellence resources later in the book.  As the excellence in your business grows, people won't mind paying more for your service or product.

# Chapter 4

# How to Find Your God-Gifted Business

**Talent vs. gift**

I didn't know the difference until I read Steve Harvey's book "Act Like a Success, Think Like a Success." Here is a snippet from the book. "*Everyone has a gift, which he defines as 'the single thing that you do at your absolute best with the least amount of effort.' A gift is beyond a job or a skill. It is something that is always present in every context. The gift might be playing sports or performing on stage, but it could also be solving problems, listening to others, working with children or even creating flower arrangements. 'Your gift is something that is connected to you whether you are working or vacationing, whether you are with the family or even all alone,' he writes. 'Your gift cannot be taken because of downsizing or given to you because someone creates a job description. Your gift exists because you do.'"*

    I finally realized what my gift was after many years of wondering. Understand that your gift is sometimes so simple that you can easily overlook it. For example, I've always known that being a hairstylist wasn't my calling. The same is true  with my food business. Other than being a  greedy eater, I wasn't a food fanatic. Even with my entertainment business, I still wondered where I fit in. I remember my mom would advise me to pick one and I couldn't seem to do it. I couldn't see myself doing any of those trades for the rest of my life or for free. After I read Steve Harvey's book, it dawned on me — those were my talents, not my gift.

    Suddenly, I was enlightened and didn't have to settle for one of my talents. Then came the real issue of discovering my gift. For years, I've asked myself what my gift is. I prayed that

God would help me realize my gift and He did. It was in my daily activities, but I'd overlooked it. People would always call me for business advice and I would get excited every time this happened. I would literally tell people all the details, both broad and personal, of how I started and sustained my businesses. As time went on, when I was asked what my hobby was or what turns me on, I would jokingly reply, "Talking about business." This is something I can do in my sleep, on my worst day and on my best day; I could do this freely for the rest of my life. You see, all the different businesses I have are extensions of my gift. My gift isn't being a hairstylist, a chef, or an entertainment executive. My gift is activating a business idea. So, what is your gift?

Your talent is something you are good at, but you have to work harder to maintain. A talent is an extension of your gift; it brings life to your gift. I'm a pretty good hairstylist, however, I work extra hard at it. I had to train harder and keep training while complaining. I enjoy doing hair and I love the smiles on my clients' faces, but I wouldn't do it for free. My mom and daughters can testify to that. With my hair business, I have to overly advertise to get customers. People are not automatically drawn to me about hair, and even if they were, I wouldn't leave a lasting impression. That's why I had to be creative to have a unique salon service. My hair salon is mobile; we provide hair services in the convenience of our customers' homes. I'm glad I have stylists like my manager, Lailla, whose gift is hairstyling. Now people will listen and take notes for hours on end when I speak about business.

And let me say this: I can talk for hours, trying to literally force people to start a business. I have repeat hair clients who come back, not just for my talent, but for my gifted talks with them. So, what are your talents? Sometimes, we have multiple talents, but they all share a common denominator: "our gifts."

Ask yourself these questions;
- What am I good or trained at? (talent)
- What do most of my friends, strangers and even my enemies compliment me on the most? (gift)
- Can I do this one thing for free for the rest of my life? (gift)
- What can I do to make an income? (talent)
- What one habit is embedded in every department of my being? (gift)

Your gift reflects in your home, relationships, job, church and so on. Most times, we overlook the gift because it's too simple. One of my sisters love music and always talks about being a musician. She also loves fashion and wants to be a fashion designer. However, I came to realize that one of her gifts is being an honest critic. That girl can size something up so accurately that it can be scary. Now, some of you might say that you hate critics since you hear criticism every day.

However, the honest critic is always appreciated and needed in life. Some of the critics we truly hate might not be gifted critics. A gifted critic like Simon Cowell will always have a fan base no matter how mean he comes off. Why? Because he is honest and functioning in his gift. My sister still battles with taming down her criticism because not everyone likes to hear the truth. However, the people around her always ask for her opinion in everything from clothes, love life, friendships and so on. I sometimes resist her criticism, but a few minutes later, I'll find myself asking her what she thinks about something. After years of me pushing her to start something that aligns with her gift, I suggested she start a fashion blog. She finally welcomed the idea and shared her gift in the fashion world. After a few weeks of posting on her social media, she tagged a fashion icon and that person commented on her post. Her operating in her gift attracted favor quickly. I gave you these examples so you won't have any confusion between the two. There's a great difference between your gifts and your talents. Discover it. You don't have to find it; it has been in you since birth.

## Gifts can have many legs

Your gift can have many extensions, meaning, you can use your gift in many fields or industries. For example, comedian Steve Harvey, can use his gift to make people laugh in different industries. He has a talk show, radio show, movies, books and so on. So, your gift is not confined only to one field of industry. It will always have many departments, because it's a part of your being. You can't use it only at work; it follows  you everywhere you go and shows up in everything you do. I'm so glad we are finally in a time where people are more welcoming to the idea of multiple streams of income. A few years back, people felt like they had to pick one gift and focus only on it. Musicians were criticized for crossing over to the movie industry and vice versa. Now, it's preached in the business world to have different extensions of your gift. I use my gift for my beauty, food and entertainment businesses. Get creative with your gift so you can have multiple streams of income. This is the key to success.

There are days when I get overwhelmed with my many legs. There are days I have to deal with various problems coming from multiple directions. A stylist may call out, a store didn't receive their order, I need to meet with my reality show editor and so on. I remember one morning going hiking and feeling stressed. I prayed and Luke 12:48 came to me. It reads, "From everyone to whom much has been given, much will be required; and from the one to whom much has been entrusted, even more, will be demanded." This brought a sense of calmness to me because I know that much has been given to me. And the Bible also says that God won't give you more than you can bear. If this isn't enough, I watched a T.D. Jakes' sermon entitled "Positioned for Favor". He taught that we are like trust funds. A trust fund is defined as "a fund consisting of assets belonging to a trust, held by the trustees for the beneficiaries." (Reference: Oxford Dictionaries/ Trust Fund). God made you a trustee of your gift, and your gift is to be shared with beneficiaries. So, why would you not share that business idea? The part of the sermon that touched me the most was when he told the story of Joseph. Joseph's gift caused him to be a slave for some time. Your gift will make you a slave some days. Stop complaining about being used for your gift and pray for the  strength that is in you. God wouldn't entrust you with that gift if you couldn't handle it. When you operate fully in your gift, making the necessary sacrifices without complaining, favor will locate you. This is what motivational speakers mean by your energy attracts what you think. That's sometimes the difference between you and your neighbor. We often ask why some people seem to attract more favor than we do. Sometimes, it's because they were operating in their gifts and we weren't. Align yourself with your gift.

## Ask the Holy Spirit

For those of you who are "mature" Christians, discovering your gift is even easier when you seek answers from the Holy Spirit. I didn't realize my gift until I grew a stronger relationship with the Holy Spirit. I had a few clues here and there, but when I could understand and hear the Holy Spirit, I started receiving clarity. I used the word "mature" for a reason. You might misinterpret what the Holy Spirit is saying if you are not "mature". Mature Christians know that the word of God (Bible) will align with what the Holy Spirit says. The Spirit won't contradict the Bible. Know the difference. It took many storms, failures, and risks for me to gain insight into my gift. Maybe if I'd had a stronger relationship with the Holy Spirit, I would have known a lot of what I know now much earlier in life. It wouldn't have been a storm-free life, but I would have focused on the promise more than the pain.  So, if you are "mature", pray and listen. He will reveal it in due season.

# Chapter 5

# Who are Your Friends?

We all have heard the sayings, "Show me your friends and I'll show you your character" and "Your environment plays a role in who you become." Some of us have scoffed at these words of wisdom, but they are true. Now, don't get me wrong — there are a few exceptional people who were born into extremely bad situations and got out of them. However, they are uncommon souls who had to endure many mental transformations to survive their environments and friends, and I believe that even these chosen few still had to create these elements in their upbringing. They had teachers and mentors who inspired them. They had situations where they had to distance themselves from what everyone else around them was doing. What I'm saying is, you can't completely escape these life principles. We have all, at some point in our lives, heard these principles from famous people. Oprah, Steve Harvey, T.D. Jakes and so on, have preached on these principles. They are not just repeating a cliched phrase. I believe a lot of life principles are shared diversely from so many mouths to ensure that people on various levels hear it. Some cliches are valuable life principles, and when life happens, we get an "aha" moment. After it happens, we start to understand what that cliché meant and it begins to resonate in our spirits.

The reason people look at your friends and judge you is simple. If most of your friends are drug addicts, you will more than likely try drugs one day. It's different when you are the only sane one trying to speak some sense into them. However, the Bible repeatedly says we should flee from sins and temptations. It says flee because the urges of our flesh are so strong that we will eventually give into them if hang around the wrong people. Oftentimes, we fool ourselves into thinking that we would never do what our friends are doing. A few weeks, months or years later, we find ourselves falling into the same traps and asking ourselves, "What was I thinking?" We weren't. So, when we only hang out with the 24/7 party-goers, we will eventually become one, not because we don't want to do better, but because that's all we know. This is because it's the only way we've learned to express ourselves or celebrate a good or bad day. In my worldly days, I promoted nightclub events. It wasn't an overnight gig and I don't regret it because it's my testimony. It started with me always clubbing. I did it and all my friends did it. Even on the days when I didn't feel like going out, I still went. Why? Because when I called every one of my friends to ask what they were doing that day, they were all going to the club. So, what was I to do? I didn't want to be stuck at home alone — bored.

Eventually,a club owner approached me and suggested we start hosting parties there in his club. This was the birth of Lionness Entertainment. We were the only African female nightclub promoters in Atlanta at that time. So, there I was suddenly having to be at the club consistently to do business. Being an African female in that business came with a stereotype. Most people in our communities assumed I was extremely promiscuous and I dressed the part. Now mind you, I was minding my business and getting paid to party. And I had never been linked or seen with someone they suspected I was romantically involved with. After years of speculations, I was asked a few times if I was gay. I got asked this because they'd investigated my romantic life and came up with nothing. I truly was minding my business, and while many others were spending money to party, I was getting paid to party. I don't say this to brag about my past because it had its repercussions. Eventually, after years of being around promiscuous friends, I did slowly become promiscuous. I would always say, "I would never do that" and question how others could do the things that they did. Before I knew it, I'd made a few bad judgments in the name of love. Eventually, after years of being my strong-minded self, a few peoples' false prophecies about me came true. I didn't flee from all the temptations around me. I convinced myself that I was more than I was and that I could handle anything. Now, when I look back, it's funny how I also slowly got out of that environment through a friend. Every time I made that infamous Friday night call and asked what she was doing, she would always say that she was going to church. "Again!" I would reply. She was the only friend of mine who was doing something different, so I would sometimes follow her lead. Initially, I didn't follow her because I was interested in church; I just wanted a different kind of party. That was the beginning of my church walk and I am forever grateful to her.

What does all this have to do with business? A lot. When you start sharing with friends about starting a business, it can make or kill your dreams. People aren't always haters; sometimes, they simply can't see or believe what you see. And I don't believe in doing things on the down-low and not tell anybody. We all need somebody to bounce ideas off and to encourage us to keep going. Your friends and family are your initial case studies. After I get a business idea, I will not start it until I talked to my ex, sister, mom and a few other people. This system has never failed me. They represent the Holy Spirit's voice in my life — in most cases. They are not my chosen board of advisers by blood titles, but because of my experience with them. Meaning your board of advisers can come from different people with different backgrounds; there's no formula to abide by. My mom, for example, didn't join that circle until I graduated college and had gained some level of success. She was so worried about my future that she couldn't clearly see or hear my present. If i wasn't talking about graduating and becoming a professional, she didn't want to hear it. After having kids of my own, I pitied the concerns I put her through because of my lack of accountability. So, your circle has to be people you selected based on your experiences with them. How did they react the last time you told them about an idea you had? Have they always had your best interest at heart? You will know who believes in you and your dreams through experience and time.

**Friends believe in you, then your dreams**

Friends aren't always people who come from a different bloodline than your own. I believe family members can become friends and friends can become family members. So, when I say "friends", I am referring to both relatives and non-relatives. True friends believe in you first, and then your dreams. This is because they may not understand the business concept clearly, even though it sounds good. Them believing in you will provoke them to encourage you regardless of how they feel about your vision. God gave you the vision, not them. When my ex first planted the seed to start *Aunties Puff Puff Mix*, I was excited. I talked to my sister and mom, but they didn't quite get it. Actually, my mom was not interested in understanding that vision. Her only vision, at that time, was me graduating from college. I spoke to my uncles and they were sold on the idea. Gradually, after I graduated college, I put together samples and everyone was excited about the concept. They didn't know how I would sell it or who would actually buy it. They were concerned because Africans love to cook from scratch, no matter the struggle. So, introducing a quick-fix food product, in their minds, would be hard. However, they believed in me, so they encouraged me and made suggestions about the packaging and flavors. Most of the people in my circle of advisers were not business owners. They knew owning a business had the potential to become a great investment, but they were afraid of risks. However, because they believed in me, they were sold on my dreams.

## You can't force a boss mentality on a working-class individual

I can't tell you how many times I have been guilty of this act. I wasn't aware that this was a problem until one of my hair clients who eventually became a friend said to me, "Louise you have to stop forcing a boss mentality on working class people." A big light bulb went off in me. I had been doing that for years, which led me to become frustrated with many of my friends. That quote started helping me in my everyday dealings, and the more I dealt with friends, the more those words of wisdom made sense to me. You see, when I discovered the business world, I was like a born-again Christian, trying to convince everyone to join the church. I was persuading everyone to start a business and enjoy the rewards. I persuaded my team members, clients, family members, church members, strangers and so on. I wanted to spread the Oprah effect. "You get a business, you get a business; everybody gets a business!" However, after the excitement fizzled, I would become frustrated. I would talk to people about how to start their businesses and give them ideas on what they needed to start with. They would be inspired and promise to finally start, but they never did. After this, I would spend countless hours counseling them on starting, giving them more ideas and encouragement. Nothing. Then, we would both get frustrated. They had all the working class excuses for why they couldn't start. Still not understanding that they were working class people, I would set up first-time gigs for them — still nothing. I was draining myself trying to forcing people to become their own bosses.

You can't help people who have these types of mindsets. If you have a great concept and you talk to them about it, they will kill it.

They will give you working-class excuses, detailing why they believe you can't do what you've set out to do. There's a difference between being in the working class, yet having a boss mentality, versus attempting to be your own boss while being bound to a working class mentality. Most people start their businesses and still have their day jobs. However, they are fully aware of where they want to be in the near future. They want to eventually stop working for someone and make the switch. So, they stop wishing and start taking the necessary steps to achieve their goals. In the beginning, those steps will not pay much, nevertheless, people with boss mentalities are sold on the idea of becoming business owners. So, they happily sacrifice, not complaining about how little money they've made. If you have a working class mentality, please transform your mind. You can't be double-minded. You have to choose a mindset and stick to it.

## Make friends in business

Making friends for networking sake is hard for me. It's a weakness that I'm still trying to work on. I remember going through my phone contacts and realizing how many potential business connections I have. My sister would ask me why I couldn't call one of those influential people for help with my ideas. I couldn't because I felt I would be bothering or trying to use them. I had potential investors, celebrities, and influential people within my reach, but I did not ask for help. Maybe if I had, I would have reduced the amount of delays and mistakes I made in my businesses. Nowadays, I try to surround myself with influential people. God uses people to help you, but you have to ask for and accept help. I wouldn't suggest you stalk people or force friendships for the sake of business. Your goal is to connect with like-minded people who will inspire you. And in return, see yourself as someone who can help them with something. It shouldn't be a one-way street in which you are the only beneficiary. Humble yourself, approach that person, offer to help them with something or send a gift. Eventually, when you have some sort of connection, ask for help. Ask without expecting to receive, so you are not disappointed if they say no. Some people get offended after they don't get the help they want from the influential people they've reached out to, or if they can't seem to reach those people. Sadly enough, they remain offended for the duration of their business's life. If you have this mindset, you will keep getting offended and miss your blessing. The people you are attempting to connect with are probably busy, have forgotten about your proposition or just don't know how to receive you. Don't take it personal; keep being kind and don't stop liking their pictures on social media. When you keep being kind, eventually you will get noticed. Even if you don't, you can still learn from those influential people via their social media pages, books or other resources.

# Chapter 6

# Where to Start

**Start in your thoughts**

Once upon a time, I had an epiphany after having a conversation with my sister. We unveiled several legs of her gift and discovered mind-blowing revelations in relation to it. It was an exciting conversation and to see how far her thoughts had changed. Most people want to know where to start a business. The where is not a specific location; it represents the numerous thoughts and fears we have with starting our own businesses. Just like everything we do in life, business starts in our thoughts or minds. Our actions are a reflection of our thoughts. So, to be able to activate and move towards our gifted businesses, we need to renew our minds. The Bible tells us in *Romans 12:2* to renew our minds. We won't be able to move a muscle without our minds telling us to do it. This is the science of the relationship between the brain and the rest of our bodily functions. Someone must first plant the seed to start in our minds before we receive the vision. There comes a season in our lives where we have to say to ourselves, "Enough is enough. I'm starting my business today." When you make up your mind to start, the rest really is history. There have been many times when I found myself counseling people who had not made up their minds to start their businesses. This was always a frustrating situation for me. I take entrepreneurship very seriously and I'm very passionate about it. So, when I'm counseling someone, I'm all in. We go over what business they can start, how to start that business, and I have even gone the extra mile and booked first-time gigs for people. This almost always led me to becoming disappointed and hurt. Yes, hurt because everyone has that one thing that makes them vulnerable and sensitive. Business is one of mine's. Some people would put pressure on me to help them start their businesses, but they would never finish setting them up or launching them. Why? Because their minds were not truly made up. When your mind is not made up, you can't flow in the creativity your gift brings. You won't see the big picture, no matter how bright I paint the wall. All you will see are obstacles and excuses.

Let's revisit the conversation I had with my sister. I realized that she couldn't see what I was talking about until she made up her mind. This is someone I talk to every day, and for years, I had been painting a great picture. She didn't see what I was seeing, and when she did see it, she didn't know how to bring it into fruition. Like I stated before, her gift, as I saw it, was being an honest critic. So, she finally started an inspirational vintage fashion page on Instagram. She didn't know what her full vision was, but I told her to just start something in alignment with her gift. After about two months, she was getting more and more creative with her page. Famous people are already commenting on her pictures and this boosted her confidence. Recently, she decided to start a fashion blog. Mind you, last year when I suggested that she start a blog, she gave me excuses. After she opened her mind to let her creative juices flow, we came up with many extensions of her Instagram page. We even discovered that she was named after a beauty product. I say this to emphasize that when you unlock your mind, you will shock yourself. The things and concepts that will flow out of your mouth will shock you. So, have you truly made up your mind?

**Too much research can be a killer**

In the age we live in, research is very important; it is key in our daily lives. We check reviews of products before we buy them. We search for the best price and so on. However, I have a different theory in regards to doing too much research. I believe that the only time research and findings are necessary to start is when you are replicating someone's business. Now, don't get me wrong, there are some businesses that have acquired some success by copying other business models. However, this book is about finding **your** true God-gifted business. When you are launching a gift-inspired business, there's no need for too much research. What do I mean by too much research? If you are constantly researching your competition, you may find yourself in a confinement. Once you discover your gift, do the right amount of research, and then start. Your research should consist of these few questions?

- Is anybody doing this business?
- What would people pay for this service or product?
- Is my business name available or already being used?
- What do I need to start and be successful in this business?

Your research should not add more reasons for you to feel incompetent. It should be about how you can start and bring your unique gift to the market. Focus your research on how to start, rather than questioning if you should start or not. When you research on how to start, you won't be distracted by how fancy your competitor is. When you research with an "if" I should start in mind, I promise you will find more reasons to not start. There's an adage that says, "Don't go looking for something bad, because you will always find it." When you do intense research with the wrong thought, it will discourage you. There will always be businesses with larger audiences, brilliant promotions and expensive presentations, but if your business idea is the first of its kind, you won't have anything to worry about. In other words, you won't be distracted. This was something I had to learn to deal with. I didn't enjoy competition back then, so I was always interested in concepts that had little to no competition. Now that I am walking in my gift, I am comfortable to add "author" to my name. There are so many authors and business books out there, but only one Louise. My gift is unique, as is yours, and will always have an audience. The fear of competition hasn't completely left my mind, but greater is He that is in me... says the Bible. There's only one you and your gift is customized for you to shine in it, regardless of how small it is. Jesus says in Matthew 17:20, *"I tell you the truth, if you had faith even as small as a mustard seed, you could say to this mountain, 'Move from here to there,' and it would move. Nothing would be impossible."*

After your thoughts are in order and you are ready to start, talk and keep talking. I have never understood the reason behind secrecy. I do understand that there's a time for talking and a time to be silent. However, people have taken secrecy to the extreme and it's killing them. God moves through people, so when you decide to never share your thoughts, who suffers? You suffer the most. Sharing not only benefits the person you are sharing with, it is also beneficial to you. Because we refuse to share and talk, we end up lacking knowledge, suffering and we don't progress. People don't want to share nowadays, even about the smallest things. I believe in sharing and talking. That's how I learned and gained knowledge. It is through sharing thoughts that I discovered my gift in business. Now, you don't have to be an open book like me; everyone is different, but by all means, share your thoughts in detail with friends, family members, and strangers. Get rid of the fear that someone will steal your idea. What is yours is yours truly. If they do steal your idea, they can't steal your gift. Your gift will allow you to innovatively express your idea. You have more to lose by not sharing. I am yet to have someone steal my idea and present it better than me. I have had numerous people and established businesses take my concept and run with it, but they have never presented it the way I did . It's comical to me now; this is, of course, after I got past the temporary anger. They have always misrepresented my vision, and it will be the same for you. Focus on your lane, share so you can gain knowledge and the Holy Spirit will speak to you through people. Sometimes, we get overwhelmed and can't listen or trust our intuition (oftentimes, the voice of the Holy Spirit). Then, when someone says something, we have an "aha" moment. You will not receive what you can't share. If you don't talk to people, ask for advice or help, it won't come to you. You have to speak to your mountains because your mountains hear only your voice.

**Start with the dream, not the money**

All successful businesses started small, never big. They either became an overnight success or gradually built their way to success. Nowadays, people have misused the phrase "go big or go home." When you start your business, it's like a newborn baby. You sacrifice for your baby without expecting your baby to say thank you, I love you or give you any other compliments. As mothers, we often envision that our kids will eventually grow up strong, respectful and make us proud. But they started as infants; keep that in mind with your new business. Let your vision drive you, not the money. When money doesn't drive you, you will likely start with low or no financial compensation. The compensation you get is that you've managed to convince one more person to give your idea a chance. With a visionary mindset, you appreciate five likes on your business's social media page photo. Starting a new business with pride will stagnate your progress. Honor your humble beginnings, and when you are in your season of success, the price of your products and services won't be an issue. I believe that's why a lot of business coaches today advise people to not garner massive amounts of debt when starting a business. That stress alone can block your creativity because it'll cause you to become overly focused on payback. Start with the little you have, or if you must borrow, borrow the bare minimum. Owing money to someone can be destructive to personalities like myself. Besides, student loans and hospital bills, I feel terrible and guilty when I owe someone. Prevent this distraction and focus on the vision. So, start with the vision and money will surely follow.

# Chapter 7

# Business Builds Confidence and Purpose

## Confidence

One of the reasons I love business is because it builds confidence. Confidence is the most sought after feeling or belief in one's lifetime. Confidence is defined as *the feeling or belief that one can rely on someone or something (Reference: Oxford Dictionaries/ confidence).* On the days you feel like a failure or you feel unattractive, owning a business will cause you to keep your confidence. Life is full of seasons, and every season has its fair share of storms. With every storm, we will go through varying measures of pain and tribulation. I realized that every time I went through a tough season in my life, my businesses kept me sane. As a matter of fact, I started and continued writing this book in the midst of my most difficult storm. I wondered why celebrities, especially singers, would always say they focused on their careers during storms. To me, this sounded very weird, because I wondered how can one's work help them through a life crisis. I believed that the person was traumatized and hurt and needed time off. The truth became clear to me after my latest and greatest storm. When you're traumatized or hurt, you lose a lot of confidence and control. Hence, focusing on something you have control over builds confidence. Now, let me explain again so we are clear that this doesn't work for every type of business; it has to be a gifted business. The business that helps you through a storm is the one that uses your gift as fuel. You don't necessarily have to be fully operating directly in your gift, but your gift should play a role in your business. Sometimes, people close their businesses during one of the storms of life, because their businesses weren't distracting them or helping them through the ordeal. This means that they were likely not operating in their gifts.

It's so amazing to me how owning a business can help during a failed relationship or depression. There were moments when my ex-husband upset me, and this upset would drive me to work harder in my business. Consequentially, I would accomplish something great, which caused me to forget about the grudge and we'll share the excitement. More than likely, you've had romantic interests who've broken your heart, but because you were operating in some measure of your gifting, you were able to keep from going insane. My ex would say the same about me. When I upset him, he would try to cool off by operating in his giftings. Being able to hear your inner self helps to reduce tension. Even if that business doesn't become financially rewarding, it will reward you tremendously. It will give you lifelong confidence. To know that you've started a business from nothing but an idea — a business that is gradually progressing is very rewarding. Your confidence will grow even on bad business days. When corporate America decides to lay you off, wouldn't it be nice to have a business to fall back on? I've always advised people — including professionals — to have a business as a backup plan. As many of us know, your boss can walk into your office any day and change your life by laying you off or firing you. Then what? You would be left feeling sorry for yourself and afraid. You can use that free time to grow your business which you had started.

## Purpose

Starting a business, most times, will reveal your purpose in life. This is because it releases your creativity and it makes you feel free. Business will humble you, especially, in the beginning. The rest is determined by a host of other factors. Most people think they have to figure out their purpose before they can start their businesses. I believe it's the other way around — as long as your gift plays a role. Any business you start that falls under the umbrella of your gift will help you gain more insight as to what your inner purpose is. You can start a business that specializes in your talent, but your gift has to have an office in that talent. This way, you are using both your gifts and your talents, and not just one. For example, as I stated earlier, hair styling is not my gift; it's a talent. However, it caused me to activate my gift of starting businesses. So, my gift has the CEO's (Chief Executive Officer) office, but my talent is the COO (Chief Operations Officer). As time went on, it became more evident to me which of the two (hair styling versus business startup) was my true gift. This became evident in the experiences and conversations I would have with my clients versus the conversations my manager, Lailla, would have with her clients. Remember, Lailla's gift is hair. My clients and I would always talk about business, while Lailla and her clients would often talk about what hair products to buy or avoid and how to treat the different textures of hair. You can see the difference, even though we were using the same talent. So, start a small business to find your inner purpose, especially if everything else isn't working.

## Maturity

I matured during the course of operating in business. It has reduced my laziness and increased my patience with people. I am not a morning person; this is something I inherited from my dad. This was one of my biggest struggles in the beginning; it's still a daily struggle to leave my blanket early in the morning. Every time I read how successful entrepreneurs woke up at sunrise, I would try to talk myself out being an entrepreneur. I was always late in the mornings. Honestly, I still run late from time to time, but it's gotten a lot better now. There's a huge difference between being one hour late versus ten minutes late, so God is still working on me. However, one of the reasons I woke up late, besides bad genes, was the fact that I hadn't realized what my gift was. I was operating only in my talent, and this wasn't giving me a strong enough pull to get out of bed. Once I realized my gift and began operating more in it, my wake up time changed from 11 in the morning to 7:30 in the morning. Praise God! Hopefully, one day I will be one of those early birds who start their days at five in the morning.

When you really want something, it'll make you want to be a better person and do whatever it is you need to do to acquire success. I started reading books that helped me, not just with business, but with life — period, and everyone who knows me, knows I don't like reading. Thank God someone hated reading just as much as I do and decided to create audiobooks. I pay my monthly Amazon Audible fees happily to have books read to me. Wanting to learn caused me to do research, and this is how I found out about audiobooks.

Information and knowledge are available all around us, but when we are not motivated to get them, we become stagnant. The Bible says in Hosea 4:6, "*My people are destroyed for lack of knowledge*". When you don't know how or what, find knowledge; don't sit around and wait for knowledge to knock on your door. It may never come knocking; you have to go get it. There's a biblical proverb that states that nothing is new under the sun. This means whatever you need knowledge on, someone has already lived it, did the research and shared the information. If it's the first time something is being done, you may not get the all of the information, but you will get enough knowledge to bring that invention to life.

You will develop maturity in dealing with people and all their different personalities. I can truly say I'm a better friend, daughter, mother, and future wife through the medium of business. Being forced to patiently and calmly deal with clients and teammates has humbled me.

Anyone who has worked in a customer service department can feel my pain. As a business owner, you don't have the luxury of just not dealing with crazy clients. You can't stop all the special customers from calling, after all, you need their business. So, you are literally forced to learn how to keep yourself calm, whether you do it through counting your breaths, prayer, talking to yourself, or so on. After years of practicing these new habits, self-calming became a trait of mine. I can now laugh when I encounter a not-so-pleasant customer or when dealing with rebellious teammates. It takes a lot to get me out of character, especially in the business world. I can't say I'm equally patient when dealing with loved ones, but it has helped.

A gifted business is like your new baby. When we have a new baby, we search for the best schools, best products and so on. We do intense research and reviews to give them the best we can. This is the same for that business idea. You need to research strategies and information that will give it the best chance of being successful.

# Chapter 8

# Business Creates a Busy Body

Being a business owner calls your attention to many different areas and departments. This is even more stressful when you are starting a business or when you become a huge success. Either way, you are needed in so many different areas. The Bible says in Luke 12:48, "To whom much is given, much is required," meaning, if you want to be that successful, creative business owner, much is required. You are required to be the marketer, laborer, salesperson, accountant, bookkeeper and so on in varying seasons. Sounds stressful, right? Yes, it is a lot to deal with. This is why most successful entrepreneurs need some spiritual element in their lives. Some choose to meditate, yoga, rituals or whatever to find peace and tranquility. God gave us the freedom of will to make choices and some have chosen to worship different gods. However, only the Prince of Peace (Isaiah 9:6), Jesus Christ, can fulfill that desire. God created us, so He knows us like no other. He knows what works for each unique individual as stated in Matthew 10:30, which reads, "And even the very hairs of your head are all numbered." So, if God knows every strand of hair on your head, then surely He knows what will bring you peace. Now I'm not saying peace means you won't have any struggles, but knowing Christ Jesus gives you peace in the midst of storms. He can speak to the storm and command peace like He did when He was in the boat with His disciples (Mark 4:39). He rebuked the storm and said, "Quiet! Be still."

### Pray and watch

Developing a praying lifestyle does not end at home or with your family. Business and prayer work like peanut butter and jelly — or for my African people — like rice and stew. We have all heard about employees, business partners, lawsuits and so on that have crushed businesses. Being a prayerful person can eliminate most of these issues. I said "can," not "might" because I have tried, reviewed and gave prayer a five-star rating. It works or you wouldn't be reading my book. I pray for the things that seem little to some people, as well as for what we believe to be major deals. Over the years and after countless business relationships, I have seen the aftermath of prayers. I even pray when I want to hire a braider for my hair company. You have to pray for everything; nothing is too little because it's in the little things that the devil creeps in. The news is always reporting stories of multi-millionaires getting sued by their assistants, stylists, janitors, and even audience members. Some of these people actually win their cases against the celebrity personalities and cause them to go broke. I always pray that God won't allow anyone to come in contact with me who is not from Him. Even if I have to hire a doorkeeper tomorrow, I will be praying for the right person. Christians especially pray for the Warren Buffett connection and forget about Mary, the housekeeper. Who do you think can cause more damage? Yes, the housekeeper who is in your personal space daily. Now, I use the housekeeper as an example, but this applies to anyone who will be working in close contact with you in your business.

One testimony I'd like to share is about the journey it took for me to hire my first administrative assistant. After years of doing business and watching my business grow, it was finally time. For two years, I constantly prayed that God would send me an assistant. It did not happen immediately, so I kept praying. At that time, I didn't have an office space outside my house. So, I was praying for an assistant without a place for the assistant to work in. When I would think about where we would be working, I would start feeling heavy. I didn't want to use my home office, after all,I barely used it as my business space. However,

I wasn't financially ready to rent an office space. Fast forward two years later during the toughest season of my life, I finally stepped out on faith and got an office. How I got the office at the price, location and timing was a testimony in and of itself. I was praying for an office and an assistant one morning when I heard the Holy Spirit telling me to go on Craigslist. Long story short, I found an office space perfect for me and moved in within two weeks. That office was space enough for exactly two desks and a lounge area. Suddenly, I found myself looking for an assistant on Craigslist, strolling through the free resume posts and that's where I met someone. I interviewed her a few days before I actually got the key to my office; she was to start the day after I moved in. I was praising God for putting all of the pieces together and my first day in the office came. The lovely assistant I had made a connection with was a no-call, no-show. I called her, but she didn't respond. I prayed, "God, what is this? You told me to go on Craigslist, and after that, I was sure I knew the voice of the Holy Spirit enough — I felt strongly about finding this person on Craigslist." After this, I told the Lord that I would try again, but this time, I paid for a business ad on Craigslist. Immediately, I was bombarded with resume after resume. As a matter of fact, I'm still receiving resumes. I got overwhelmed because I'm the type of person who becomes double-minded when I have too many options. Even when I go to a restaurant, I hate menus that have a lot of options. Now, the same day I posted the business ad, I received a text from a hair client of mine who happened to be looking for a job and saw my ad. She sent me a text, saying that she was interested. I got excited and started praising God again. I shared the good news with my sister, who advised me to still look into the other candidates. This is why I stated earlier that you need to be accountable to wise counselors. Being secretive will harm you. I took my sister's advice, and she was right because my client didn't follow through. So, the next day, I prayed before going through the resumes. I did some research online on how to hire. Yes, I did my homework. Prayer is good, but you still need to do some research. You have to still do the work that is required. After doing a little research, I put a list of questions and strategies together. I went through the resumes and created an A-list and B-list. I made calls to the A-list first and fell in love with two of the candidates. After a few calls, I stopped worrying about the B-list. So again, I got excited and spoke to a few of my wise counselors, asking which candidate I should pick. I was leaning towards a candidate who I'd spoken to when my energy was calm, and I really liked how sweet and mellow she sounded. She was my first choice, and we scheduled an interview for the next Monday. I scheduled interviews for Monday and Tuesday with all four candidates from my A-list. Monday arrived and I came to my office wearing a new outfit I'd bought purposely for that day, and NO one showed up. My two best candidates didn't show up, even my friend who was to be my helper didn't show up. I felt so rejected that I closed the office early, went home in tears and drowned myself in a jar of Talenti ice cream. I prayed, "God, what am i missing?" And I heard this word clearly: "wait". The next day, I remembered that I had one candidate who I hadn't really felt connected to on the phone, so I didn't expect her to show up, but she did. What's more is she was 15 minutes early, had her two kids in the car with her, and the interview went great. She wanted the job so much that she'd brought her kids and her mother to the interview with her. Again, I got excited and texted my spiritual dad about the good news. As soon as I finished praising the Lord, another candidate walked in the door, ready to be interviewed for the job. Still to this day, I don't recall setting that time with her. Right after she showed up, my friend showed up to help with the interview process. She was the one who'd forgotten to come the previous day, but she was on time this day. Apparently, I'd given both of them the same time on Tuesday. I prayed, "God, what is this? I've already promised this job to the previous candidate." I started telling my friend that this is confusing to me because I'd already hired someone. So, we still had to interview the candidate who, ironically enough, ended being perfect for my friend who is also a business owner. I spent the entire interview asking the candidate questions that I knew my friend would ask, even down to, "Do you like dogs?" The Holy Spirit was just all up in there and we were both in awe of Him. He is a master strategist, and He never fails.

I gave this long testimony to point out what I learned after being excited four times before getting the one. Matthew 26:41 says, "Watch and pray so that you will not fall into temptation. The spirit is willing, but the flesh is weak." After you pray, watch people's actions and character. Don't get too excited and forget to still put people through a process. This is your business, so if you feel that a connection alone will take your business to the next level, it might not. People have to show up and show out — no excuses. I don't care if you are my fellow church member or family member, you have to go through my business process and pass to be considered. Feelings alone don't cut it, but feelings and work ethic are matches made in Heaven. God will send you people who will show up and show out. So, don't compromise; whatever process you had in place before encountering a prospect, follow through with that system. And know that when we pray for things, most of the time, the enemy will send counterfeits our way. You have to keep praying through the process to make sure it is God-sent, not a counterfeit. I am learning daily to not only focus on my feelings, but to trust God and know that He is a God of excellence.

A praying business owner = a less stressful business owner.

# Chapter 9

# Balancing Life with Business

In this present day and age, balancing the demands of everyday life has been one of our greatest obstacles. We all want to be that person who has and keeps it all together. Countless techniques, businesses, business gurus, speakers and so on have surfaced in an effort to solve this dilemma. With all the available apps, electronics, quick fixes, books and much more, our generation is still more stressed out than ever in history. I have to come to believe that we all need to get back to a principles-centered life. I gathered this knowledge from *Stephen Covey's, book "7 Habits of Highly Effective People."* I  am making daily efforts to implement these habits into my life. I highly recommend you to read this book and let it minister to you. Let's take an overview of the habits:

1. Be proactive, not reactive.
2. Begin with the end in mind.

3. Put first things first.
4. Think win-win.
5. Seek first to understand, then to be understood.
6. Synergize.
7. Sharpen the saw.

If you really think about it, the points I shared are all common knowledge that most of us have heard before, plus, they are biblical. However, few of us put them into practice; I'm guilty of this as well. As Mr. Covey explains, living a life based on principles will help you to become more effective in everything you do. Let's dive into each trait a bit more.

**Habit 1:** Be proactive, not reactive. I have fallen short of this habit many times and suffered the consequences. Thank God for second, third and many chances. Our lives, whether personal or business, should be a product of our decisions, not our emotions. In doing business, you will encounter people, opportunities, and moments that can define your business. This is critical, especially in the beginning of your business because it defines your business. There will be rude clients who you will have to refrain from responding to. There will be opportunities that look like doors opened by God Himself, but closer inspection of those doors will keep you from walking through them. There will be moments when you'll have to think and pray before you make a decision or promise. There will be fights and disagreements that you'll need to walk away from. The Bible states, "*I call heaven and earth to witness against you today, that I have set before you life and death, blessing and curse. Therefore choose life, that you and your offspring may live*" (Deuteronomy 30:19 ESV). In life and business, we cannot control what happens or is being done to us. However, we have the authority and control over how we choose to respond. So, choose life abundantly or you will have to suffer the inescapable consequences.

**Habit 2:** Begin everything with the end in mind. Before starting a business, have a vision of the end. What do you want clients, employees, and partners to say about your business? Mr. Covey says we should imagine the day of our funerals. What would you want people to say about you? What legacy do you want to leave behind for your children? Proverbs 13:22 reads, "A good man leaveth an inheritance to his children's children: and the wealth of the sinner is laid up for the just." Set your principles now before you get started, and stick with them. I remember when I started Mobile Braiders, I braided on Sundays. When I added other stylists on my team, we had Sundays available. However, when I started to strengthen my walk with Christ, things changed. I enjoyed my time in church on Sundays and family outings thereafter. So, I made a decision that I wasn't going to work on Sundays. However, the other stylists could work if they chose to. Wrong choice. Even though I wasn't working, I would get calls from stylists about Sunday appointments. I could not concentrate at church, so I had to make a decision. After learning that Chick-fil-A, a multi-million company, closed on Sundays to observe the holy day, I made an executive decision that my company was not going to be open on Sundays either. This was one of the many principles I wanted to live by, and I have done so happily. So, what principles do you want your company to live by?

**Habit 3:** Put first things first. As the CEO, you have to decide what's first in your company. Do clients come first? Or do employees, sales, character, family, creativity, and so on take high priority? This is a question you need to answer because it structures your business's mission statement. And there is no right or wrong choice, choose what will work for you. For example, if your customers are first, you should have a team and process that keeps them first. This helps to guide your hiring process and it helps with the business partnerships you choose. So, please don't put your preferences before your priorities. If you do, you will wake up one-day and not be able to recognize yourself.

**Habit 4:** Think win-win. Yes, there is space in the business world for everyone to win. I know we might believe that in order for our businesses to succeed, our competitors have to suffer. This is not the case; there's enough space in the world for us all to profit. This is where collaboration plays a beneficial role. Collaboration with the right partners can be highly profitable to your business. So, when you encounter someone in a similar field or target market, collaborate, instead of trying steal their social media followers or clients for your sole profit. I love and agree with this African proverb, which says, " You eat; I eat." In other words, if I help your business grow, I will automatically reap the benefits, regardless of how you treat me. It's all in how you look at the outcome.

**Habit 5:** Seek first to understand, and then to be understood. In other words, listen before you speak. I love to talk, and I mean a lot! As I grow older, I have started learning how to stop putting my foot in my mouth. Don't get me wrong, I haven't stopped talking a lot, I just try to listen just as much as I talk. God is still working on me in that area. Now, some people hate talking, and for this reason, they shut down and just listen. In his book *7 Habits of Highly Effective People, Stephen Covey clearly states,* "Listen to understand, then to be understood." Communication is a two-way road; you need to first be understood before you speak and ask questions when you don't understand something. I personally prefer communicating with people who are talkative versus people who are unresponsive. Nothing gets resolved when communication is lacking.

**Habit 6:** Synergize.Dictionary.com defines the word communicate this way: *to work or act with another or other persons willingly and agreeably.* I love this principle because it speaks to my creative side. Mr. Covey teaches about valuing and celebrating differences. I love when I read about multi-million companies whose headquarters have a fun culture. Company cultures that allow employees to be themselves create positive work environments. I personally couldn't work in a corporate office setting where everyone is expected to be the same. A great culture is established when different personalities and backgrounds come together and create something phenomenal. Appreciate the differences in your teammates, hiring process and partnerships. This is where everyone's true gift is appreciated and used to its maximum capacity. Don't just hire or work with people who talk, walk, think and react like you. Synergize!

**Habit 7:** Sharpen the saw. Life is an everlasting school; we should never get to a place in our lives where we believe we know it all. There is always something to educate yourself on. Successful, rich people keep gaining knowledge through research and education. You do this to renew your mind, create better strategies, and sharpen your skills. Romans 12:2 says, "Do not conform to the pattern of this world, but be transformed by the renewing of your mind." How do you renew your mind daily? By monitoring what you hear, see, read and talk about every day, especially in the mornings. Feed yourself daily with information that renews and transforms you. Cultivate a morning routine with principles that you want to live by. I had to stop checking my phone, social media, text messages and emails as soon as I woke up. As a matter of fact, I don't talk to certain friends or relatives early in the morning. Why? Because words that are not positive or Godly would stay in my spirit all day and interrupt my productive thoughts. So, I don't engage in small-talk in the morning; I wait until I've had a productive day.

# Chapter 10

# Money and Finances in Business

## Educate yourself

Let's face it, some of us were raised with bad money habits. For some of us, our parents did the best they knew, so we can't blame them. However, we have no excuse to stay ignorant of financial knowledge. Whatever you are going through financially, someone has been there, made it through it and wrote a book about it. Find that book, YouTube video or blog, and gain knowledge. The Bible says, "My people are destroyed from lack of knowledge" ( Hosea 4:6). When I look back at all the mistakes I suffered  through due to lack of knowledge, I shake my head in dismay because the answers were literally a Google search away. I communicate with people daily and I'm amazed at the lack of knowledge we have. In this age of the internet, there's almost nothing you can remain ignorant of if you seek knowledge. People get taken advantage of financially because of lack of knowledge. There are companies out there that charge people hundreds of dollars to help them register their businesses, and I can't say they are fraudulent because people sign up for them without doing any research. There are many successful companies preying on people who lack knowledge. It's time to say enough is enough and do whatever work we have to do to help our businesses grow. Research and educate yourself on how to handle your unique financial situation. Don't be reactive when financial decisions arise; be proactive.

Take online or onsite financial classes if you need to improve your finances. Read books written by other successful entrepreneurs. Do research online and talk to others about ways to cut costs, how to market on a budget, bookkeeping, accounting and so on. Stay updated.

## Don't chase the money, chase service

This is a statement I had been hearing and it didn't resonate with me until recently. The more I grew in business and wisdom, the more it made sense. Don't chase the money; just do the best you can and money will chase you. Some of you have probably heard this statement in some form or another, and it is true. Yes, of course, we all want to make money; we want money to be attracted to us. However, the best way to attract money is through good service. That way, people will value their relationship with you versus their relationship with the product or service you're selling.  No one can replace you, but people can sell the same products and services that you're selling. Think about it for just a moment. There are some companies or brands that you have bought into because of their great customer service alone. You could have used another company that has better products, but you stuck with that particular company because of their customer service. Good customer service keeps your business in business. Of course, we know that there are companies that have horrible service but great products, and they still make money. Nevertheless, they normally don't stay in business long. My point is good customer service gives longevity to a business and creates a longstanding legacy. The best formula to a successful company is great customer service plus good products and/or services. When these two come together, they attract money and success. Please note that success doesn't necessarily mean you make a certain amount of money; success is creating and maintaining a legacy you can live with and be proud of.

Great customer service will always speak for you. Someone will be inspired to share your service ethics. I once heard a person say that your gift will bring you in front of great men, but your great service or character will keep you there. In other words, you will attract clients because you are gifted in a particular craft, however, how you treat them will determine if they stay or leave. I can tell you that I have seen this in my own business. People like to feel special, and when your product or service accomplishes this, you win. They become addicted to your brand. Nowadays, people are smarter and don't like marketers or sales people who make repeated attempts to sell them something. For this reason, most companies have realized that we (as a whole) need to go back to the basics. Serving the people in order to draw them in to spend money is a bad business move. This is why many companies have free trials and offers that are beneficial to their potential clients. The days when a salesman would walk up to a potential client and say, "Hey, do you want to buy this great product?" are gone. Nowadays, salespeople lure customers in by offering an added value to the service or product they're offering. And how genuine you are when you do this will determine how successful you are. Customers are smart; they won't fall for manipulation. So, if your product is great, and you believe it adds value to someone, sell the value, not the product. So when in doubt, just start it!

# Glossary

# Helpful Glossary Resources

**Fiverr App** - freelance app to hire and outsource graphics, branding, marketing and so much, starting at $5.

**Office Depot** - same day printing in large quantities, such as labels for product, posters, banners, etc.

**UPS Business Account** - create a business account to get a huge discount on shipping. It is free!

**Secretary of State Business License** - register your business online in minutes.

**Department of Agriculture** - Get a food license for products, catering, etc.

**Uline.com packaging** - packaging, boxes, bags, and so much more.

**Aliexpress/Alibaba** - Buy directly from factories in china and sell.

**Social Media Marketing and Presence -** facebook/instagram/pinterest ads

**Library Meeting Rooms** - your local library has meeting rooms available to be used for free. Host business events or team meetings.

**Paypal and Square accounts, swipers** - make it easy to receive any method of payment. Card, online, text or app.

**Canva.com** - create any graphics yourself for free. Flyers, social media graphics, book cover, etc

**MailChimp** - free mass marketing and automatic emails to easily communicate with customers.

**Udemy** - take online courses in any subject you lack knowledge in.

**YouTube** - university of YouTube is what I call it. You can learn anything on this platform. If you have a question, search for a video on YouTube.

**Amazon Audible** - Gain knowledge by listening to audiobooks. Great for people like me who hate reading or don't have the time to read. Listen to a book while driving or working out.